PETS' GUIDES

# Slinky's Guide to
# Caring for Your
# Snake

Isabel Thomas

Chicago, Illinois

© 2015 Heinemann Library,
an imprint of Capstone Global Library, LLC
Chicago, Illinois

Edited by James Benefield and Brynn Baker
Designed by Cynthia Akiyoshi
Picture research by Tracy Cummins
Production by Victoria Fitzgerald
Originated by Capstone Global Library Ltd
Printed and bound in China by RR Donnelley Asia

18 17 16 15 14
10 9 8 7 6 5 4 3 2 1

**Library of Congress Cataloging-in-Publication Data**

Thomas, Isabel, 1979- author.
  Slinky's guide to caring for your snake / Isabel
Thomas.
      pages cm.—(Pets' guides)
  Summary: "In this book, Slinky the Snake
reveals how readers should go about choosing
a pet snake, what supplies they will need, how
to make a new snake feel at home, and how to
properly care for a pet snake, including feeding,
exercising, and keeping a snake vivarium
clean. Text is accompanied by clear, labeled
photographs to further reinforce key concepts,
and the use of an animal narrator also allows the
book to be used to teach perspective"—Provided
by publisher.
  Includes bibliographical references
and index.

ISBN 978-1-4846-0263-8 (hardcover)
ISBN 978-1-4846-0270-6 (paperback)
ISBN 978-1-4846-0286-7 (eBook PDF)

1. Snakes as pets—Juvenile literature. I. Title.
SF459.S5
    639.3'96—dc23            2013040455

**Acknowledgments**
We would like to thank the following for
permission to reproduce photographs:
Alamy: © Juniors Bildarchiv GmbH, 13, 14, © ZUMA
Press, Inc., 7; Capstone Library: Karon Dubke, 5,
11, 20, 25, 26; Getty Images: John Cancalosi, 18,
Russell Illig, 8; Shutterstock: Joel Kempson, 16,
Willie Davis, front cover; Superstock: imagebroker.
net, 23; Design Elements Shutterstock: iBird,
Picsfive, R-studio

We would like to thank Alan H. Wilkie for his
assistance in the preparation of this book.

Every effort has been made to contact copyright
holders of material reproduced in this book. Any
omissions will be rectified in subsequent printings
if notice is given to the publisher.

007013RRDF14 .

# Contents

Some words are shown in bold, **like this**. You can find out what they mean by looking in the glossary.

# Do You Want a Pet Snake?

Howdy! I'm Slinky and this book is about pet snakes like me. Did you know that some snakes make great pets? It's amazing to watch us and learn how we live.

Snakes are **reptiles**, and we need special care. Before getting a pet snake, be sure you can look after me properly. I'll need a safe, clean place to live, the right kind of food, places to hide and explore, and **vet** care if I get sick or injured.

# Choosing Your Snake

You will need expert help to choose a snake. Corn snakes like me are some of the most common pet snakes. We have beautiful colors and patterns. Milk snakes, rat snakes, and king snakes are often kept as pets, too. Ask the expert if I'm supposed to feel smooth or rough. This will help you know if I'm ill.

Some snakes are too big to be kept as pets. Look at this python! It is kept in special conditions, in a zoo!

Find out how long I will live and how big I will get. Make sure that you will be able to give me enough space as I grow. Some snakes grow much too big to be kept as pets.

I am happy to be kept as a pet because I was born in **captivity**. Never buy a snake that has been taken from the wild. The best places to get a pet snake are good **breeders**, **animal shelters,** and **rescue centers**.

A healthy snake has bright eyes, smooth skin, and a flicking tongue. Ask to see its feeding and **shedding** record, too. This is where an owner writes down how well a snake eats and sheds its skin.

# Getting Ready

Your snake will live in a special tank called a **vivarium**. Ask a vet or an expert that knows all about snakes to help you choose the right type. My vivarium will need to be at least as long as me, so I can stretch out. Remember, I will need more space as I grow!

The temperature and **humidity** inside the vivarium must be right. They should match your snake's wild **habitat**. Set up my home at least a week before I move in. Check the temperature and humidity often. If it's too hot, I can die! You can use a **thermostat**.

Don't forget the furniture! I will need:

- rough rocks to help me shed my skin
- hiding places at the warm and cool ends of my vivarium
- branches for climbing. Buy specially cleaned branches from a pet shop.

Snakes spend lots of time **basking** in the heat and cooling off in the shade, but we like exploring, too. Change my furniture every so often so I don't get bored. You could make new hiding places out of cardboard tubes, boxes, or plant pots.

# Welcome Home

When my vivarium is ready, it's time to bring me home. Small snakes can be carried in a plastic box with a lid. Make sure the box has air holes and doesn't get too warm or too cool. Larger snakes need a cotton bag tied tightly at the top.

Find out how many hours of light and darkness your snake needs. Corn snakes like me like it to be light when the sun is up and dark when the sun goes down. Snakes are very good at escaping. Attach the vivarium lid tightly, and make sure there are no holes.

# Feeding Time

Most pet snakes eat **rodents**, such as mice or small rats. Pet shops sell frozen rodents that are just the right size for my mouth. I can swallow a meal one and a half times the size of my head. Gulp!

Snakes don't need breakfast, lunch, and dinner. Most grown-up snakes only need one meal a week. Feed me outside my vivarium, so I don't eat my bedding by mistake. I also need clean drinking water in a heavy bowl so it won't tip over.

# Shedding

Snakes shed their scaly skin as they grow. You can watch me do this several times a year. My skin goes dull and I move around less. My eyes look cloudy and I may not want to eat. Please don't touch me while I'm shedding.

Give me a large water bowl to soak in, and make sure I have rocks to rub my head on. When I've finished shedding, take the old skin away. Gently remove any old skin left on my body.

# Handling

Snakes can be shy, and we don't like to be handled very often. Try not to pick me up more than three or four times a week.

- Wash your hands before and after you handle me.

- Move slowly and be gentle.

- Support my whole body using both hands.

- Hold me loosely so I can move through your hands without getting hurt.

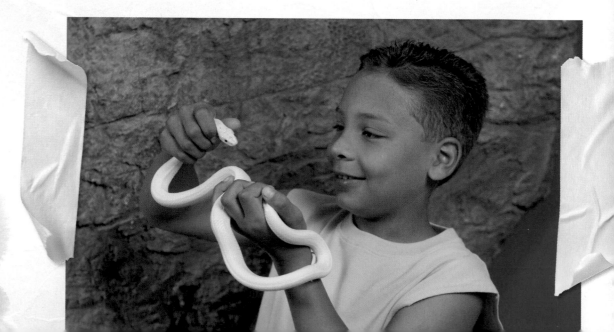

**X** Never touch me just after touching my food. I might think your hand is my next meal.

**X** Never handle me after I've eaten. I might be sick. Wait two days.

**X** Never handle me when I'm shedding.

**X** Don't kiss me or put me near your mouth.

# Keeping Me Healthy

Write down when I eat and shed my skin. You could record my weight and length, too. A healthy snake eats, sheds, and grows well. If you spot any signs of sickness, take me to visit a vet who knows a lot about snakes.

## Slinky's Health Check:

- Check my tongue. Is it flicking in and out quickly, tasting the air? The ends should not be stuck together.

- Check my body. Does it feel firm?

- Check my skin. It should not have any blisters or lumps. Can you see any **mites**?

- Check my nostrils. Do I have a runny nose? Am I having trouble breathing?

# Cleaning My Home

Snakes need clean homes to stay healthy, so check my vivarium every day. Make sure the temperature and humidity are just right. Take away any damp or dirty bedding. Change the water in my water bowl, especially if I've taken a bath in it.

You will need to clean the whole vivarium about once a month. While you're cleaning, keep me in my traveling box or bag. Use special cleaning products that are safe for reptiles. Rinse everything and make sure it is completely dry before you put me back in.

# Help from Other People

If you would like to keep a pet snake, you will need help from other people. Ask experts to help you choose the right snake. Find a vet nearby who knows about caring for snakes. You will also need a grown-up to help you care for your snake at home.

When you go on vacation, teach someone else how to look after me while you are away. They will need to visit every day to keep my vivarium clean and check that I'm happy and healthy. Don't forget to send me a postcard!

# Snake Facts

- There are nearly 3,000 different types of snakes. Not all snakes make good pets.

- Most snakes eat meat. Some eat fish, insects, and bird eggs. Before you get a pet snake, find out what it eats.

- Most snakes like to live on their own, but some can be kept in small groups.

- Anacondas are the world's largest snakes. They can grow up to 33 feet (10 meters) long. They do not make good pets.

# Slinky's Top Tips

- Watch me carefully if I'm sick after eating. I may be unwell or unhappy.

- Ask a vet or reptile expert to help you choose a pet snake, find a good breeder, and learn how to care for your new pet.

- Never touch snakes that you spot in the wild. They could be dangerous.

- If you already have pet snakes, **quarantine** your new pet to make sure it doesn't have an illness it could pass on to the others.

# Glossary

**animal shelter** organization that cares for animals that do not have homes

**basking** lying in a warm or bright place

**breeder** person who helps animals have babies in an organized way

**captivity** kept by humans instead of living in the wild

**habitat** natural home of a wild animal

**humidity** how much water vapor there is in the air

**mite** tiny spider-like bugs that lives on larger animals

**quarantine** keeping a new pet away from other animals to make sure it does not pass on an illness

**reptile** type of animal with scaly skin that usually lays eggs with soft shells

**rescue center** organization that rescues animals that are lost, injured, or not being taken care of properly

**rodent** type of animal with front teeth that never stop growing, such as mice and rats

**shedding** losing the top layer of old skin

**thermostat** device that controls how hot or cold it is in a room or an enclosure, such as a vivarium

**vivarium** special home for a pet where the temperature and other conditions can be made to match what it would be like in the wild

**vet** person trained to care for ill or injured animals

# Find Out More

## Books

Armentrout, David and Patricia. *Slithering Snakes and How to Care For Them* (Let's Talk about Pets). Rourke Publishing, 2011.

Morgan, Sally. *Lizards and Snakes* (Pets Plus). Mankato, Minn.: Smart Apple Media, 2013.

## Websites

Learn more about snake safety at:
**http://humanesociety.org/animals/snakes**

Learn more about caring for pet snakes at:
**http://petmd.com/reptile/petcare**

# Index